Heritage W in the London Borough of Enfield

Exploring six areas of historic and architectural interest

Forty Hill and Bulls Cross, Enfield Town, Edmonton, Enfield Lock, Southgate and Winchmore Hill

Edited by Monica Smith and
Enfield Preservation Society

Designed and produced by Mike Hazeldine

Published by
Enfield Preservation Society
Jubilee Hall, 2 Parsonage Lane, Enfield, EN2 0AJ

Registered charity No. 276451

ISBN   13: 978 0 907318 19 4

British Library Cataloguing in Publication Data. A catalogue
record for this book is available from the British Library.

Contents

Foreword

I have enjoyed a close working relationship with Enfield Preservation Society for more than thirty years and I cannot find words adequate to praise its efforts both to preserve Enfield's heritage and promote interest in Enfield's history.

The latest publication is of the usual high standard that we have come to expect from Enfield Preservation Society. Anyone with even the slightest interest in Enfield's history will find something to enjoy. The glories of Gentleman's Row and Forty Hill are well known but it may come as a surprise to some readers to learn that there are other parts of the borough equally worthy of attention.

This booklet is more than worthy of a place on Enfield bookshelves.

Graham Dalling,
Local History Officer

Acknowledgments

This booklet is the result of cooperation between Enfield Preservation Society and Southgate District Civic Trust. Our thanks are especially due to those members of both societies who provided text and illustrations. (A note about both societies will be found at the back of the booklet).

We are grateful to Graham Dalling, London Borough of Enfield Local History Officer who has been so helpful about so many of our publications, for checking the accuracy of the text and writing the Foreword.

Special thanks are due to the following:
      Peter Hodge for making available the text of the Southgate and Winchmore Hill walks.
      Phil Briers, Peter A.J. Brown and Alan Skilton –
      for permission to reproduce their drawings.
      Geoffrey Bone for drawing the Southgate and Winchmore Hill maps.
      Additional illustrations and maps by Peter Garland.
      Cover photograph by Stanley R. Smith.

Without the contributions of all the above we would not have been able to produce this booklet.

Monica Smith

Introduction

You will notice references to the following in the text:

CONSERVATION AREAS. Each of the six walks includes at least one of the fifteen designated conservation areas in the London Borough of Enfield. Legislation gives local planning authorities the power to ensure that any new building in such areas is sympathetic to its surroundings. It also controls the demolition of buildings and the felling of trees. The main aim is to protect the special character of each area and to ensure that when changes are made, the quality of the heritage is maintained.

LISTED BUILDINGS. Such buildings are protected by English Heritage on behalf of the Government because of their special architectural or historic importance. Records of the 379,000 listed buildings in England are kept by English Heritage and can be viewed on *www.imagesofengland.org.uk*. They also deal with recommendations for additions to the list. Where buildings seen during these walks are listed, this is noted in the text. The grades of listing are:

Grade 1 – of paramount importance
Grade 11* – of outstanding interest
Grade 11 – of special interest.
Group Value – GV follows the grade where buildings form an important architectural or historic unity or a fine example of planning (for example squares, terraces and model villages)

Churches were originally listed A (equivalent to Grade 1), B (Grade 11*) and C (Grade 11). They are being re-listed and so you will find examples of both grading systems in the booklet.

Local interest – these buildings are on a list compiled by the local authority. This offers less statutory protection than the national system.

OPEN HOUSE LONDON – Every year, normally the third weekend in September, some buildings not usually open to the public, offer free access. Details from mid-August at *www.openhouse.org.uk* or Information Line 09001 600 061. Some places mentioned in the walks are often open during this weekend only.

PLAQUES. You will note different types on the walks. Of particular interest are **BLUE PLAQUES** on buildings where famous people lived, worked or studied.

English Heritage Blue Plaque   *EPS Bronze Plaque*

BRONZE PLAQUES for listed buildings in Enfield – produced by Enfield Preservation Society.

INFORMATION

Length of walk. Each walk can take between one and a half and two and a half hours, depending upon how much time is spent looking at each building.

Refreshments are available along all the routes at public houses and cafes.

Transport. The starting and finishing points of all walks are served by public transport.

Map references. Numbers on the map refer to the item highlighted in the paragraph with that number.

Walk No. 1 –
Forty Hill & Bulls Cross

1. Gough Park
2. The Hermitage
3. Worcester Lodge
4. The Dower House

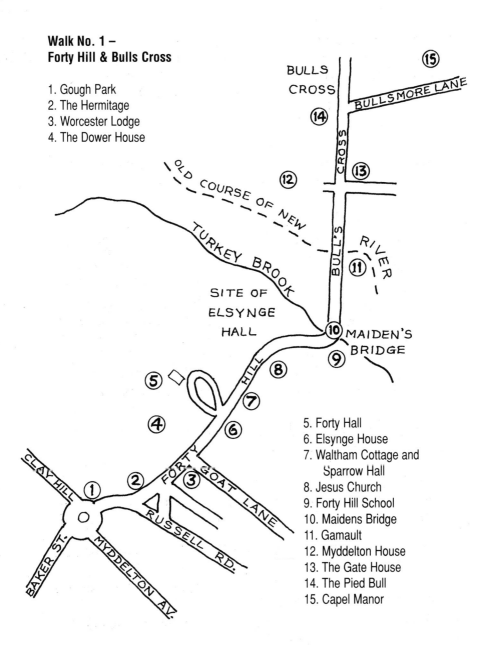

5. Forty Hall
6. Elsynge House
7. Waltham Cottage and Sparrow Hall
8. Jesus Church
9. Forty Hill School
10. Maidens Bridge
11. Gamault
12. Myddelton House
13. The Gate House
14. The Pied Bull
15. Capel Manor

Heritage Walk No. 1
Forty Hill and Bulls Cross

The ancient hamlets of Forty Hill and Bulls Cross with part of Forty Hall Estate make up the Forty Hill Conservation Area. The Roman road to Lincoln, Ermine Street, ran through it. By the end of the 16th century the settlements were well established and dominated by Elsynge Hall. This was originally a timber-framed building, replaced by a brick one in 1487 and demolished c.1656. By this date the area had begun to attract the London gentry and Forty Hall (see para. 5) and the Dower House (see para. 4) had been built between 1630 and 1640 as were many more fine houses in the next hundred years. Most of them can be seen in the course of this walk. The Bowles family, key figures in Enfield life for over a century, were particularly associated with this area, living at Myddelton House and Forty Hall. Although close to Enfield Town, this part of the borough remains surprisingly rural with a rich variety of buildings.

1. Begin the walk at the junction of Baker Street.and Myddelton Avenue and take the pedestrian path towards Forty Hill. Immediately on your left you will see the early 18th century **GATE AND BRICK WALLS TO GOUGH PARK** (Grade II). This is all that remains of the entrance to the residence of Richard Gough, an antiquarian. The house was demolished in 1899.

2. Continue up the pathway to the former GOAT PUBLIC HOUSE, built in 1929 in mock Tudor style, now being converted into flats. Within living memory this triangular area of greensward was the village pond. Old Forge Road is a reminder that the village smithy stood here, complete with chestnut tree, until 1931. Opposite the green is No.78 **THE HERMITAGE** (Grade II*), a glorious house in local red brick, acknowledged as a perfect example of its date

The Hermitage

(1704). Behind the handsome front are two timber-framed Tudor cottages which have been skilfully incorporated into the house, The adjacent COTTAGE PLACE (Grade II), Nos.70-76, is an attractive example of artisan housing (1833).

3. Walk up Forty Hill on the right hand side to No. 29, a late Georgian villa on the corner of Old Forge Road. Its fancied resemblance to a tea canister is recognised in its name CANISTER LODGE (Local interest). No. 35, **WORCESTER LODGE** (Grade II) on the south side of Goat Lane, dates from 1704 and has moulded wooden eaves. It was the home of the Rev, Samuel Joseph Smith, minister of Baker Street Chapel (Congregational) and for some years the manse of the

Worcester Lodge

10

Baptist chapel. On the opposite corner of Goat Lane stands the old GOAT HOUSE, the former Goat Inn.

4. Cross the road and continue until you see a kissing gate. The drive adjacent to this gate leads to the **DOWER HOUSE** (Grade II), formerly part of the Forty Hall Estate. Built in the early 1600s, the house contains a remarkable painted mural (c.1640) which was uncovered above a fireplace. The house has been converted into two dwellings, the other one being called Atherton House.

5. Back in Forty Hill go through the ENTRANCE GATEWAY (Grade II), built c.1800. Go ahead on the path towards **FORTY HALL** (Grade I) and note the splendid Atlantic Cedar on your left. This is a magnificent Jacobean mansion, built between 1629 and 1632 for Sir Nicholas Raynton, who was Lord Mayor of London in 1632. The style is unusually progressive for its date and the interior has some original plaster ceilings, a panelled room and an early screen in the dining room. In 1895 it was bought by Mr. Henry Carington Bowles of Myddelton House for his eldest son

Gateway to Forty Hall Courtyard

and remained a Bowles family home until it was sold to Enfield Urban District Council in 1951 for £43,000. The house is now a museum and art gallery and it is normally open to the public, free of charge, from Wednesdays to Sundays. To the west of the front door a rectangular court-yard can be seen through a spectacular gateway with high wrought iron gates. It is flanked by the former STABLE RANGE (Grade II) which has been converted into a banqueting

Forty Hall

suite. Some of the old farm buildings can be seen to the west of the house, including Grade II listed barns which are being restored by Capel Manor College. Beneath the meadows to the north of the Hall lie the remains of Elsynge Palace, occupied by Sir Thomas Lovell from 1492 and later a royal residence, especially associated with the children of Henry Vlll.

6. Leave the Forty Hall grounds by the Entrance Gateway and cross the road to observe three interesting houses: **ELSYNGE HOUSE AND ELSYNGE COTTAGE, LONGBOURN and FORTY HILL HOUSE** are all 18th century buildings and listed Grade II.

7. Continue to just beyond the drive to Clock House Nursery where you will see **WALTHAM COTTAGE** (Grade II) **and SPARROW HALL** (Grade II), both 18th century structures which have been substantially rebuilt. Sparrow Hall was originally a farmhouse but was enlarged to become the vicarage of Jesus Church. Note the unusually tall ginko tree in the front garden.

8. After passing the modern vicarage you will come to **JESUS CHURCH** which was built in 1835 as a "Chapel of Ease" to St. Andrew's Parish Church but in 1845 it became a parish church in its own right. The building was endowed by the then owner of Forty Hall, Christian Meyer because, so the story goes, his family had become reluctant to walk into Enfield Town for Sunday worship. The original church was an almost exact copy of Holy Trinity Church, Tottenham.

Jesus Church

9. Passing the church meadow to the right you come to **FORTY HILL SCHOOL** (Local interest). This was built in 1851 at a cost of £909 9s. 8d. and is the oldest junior school still in use in Enfield. Although it has been modernised and extended some original features such as the latticed windows remain.

10. Beyond the school the road crosses Turkey Brook by Maidens Bridge into Bulls Cross. This was built in 1761 but it is known that there was a bridge in place by 1572. **Nos 4-7 MAIDENS BRIDGE** (Grade II) form a row of picturesque cottages on the right. Particularly interesting is the former single classroom INFANTS SCHOOL (Local interest), built by James Meyer of Forty Hall in 1848 and used as a school until his death in 1894. It is now part of cottage No.3.

11. The straightness of the road from this point shows it follows the line of the Roman Ermine Street which continued north into Hertfordshire. At the brow of the hill the road crosses the original course of the NEW RIVER. The form of the bridge arches can still be seen at road level in the high brick walls on either side. The New River was constructed by Sir Hugh Myddelton in 1610-13 to carry drinking water from natural springs at Amwell along a 40-mile man-made channel. The modern river, which is still in use, is shorter and straighter than the first. The loop which flowed under the road and through the gardens of Myddelton House has been filled in. Thames Water, the owner of the New River, has constructed a tunnel just south of Maidens Bridge to divert the flow into the London ring main system. By the end of 17th century control of the New River Company had passed to a Huguenot family who gave their name to a formidable Victorian house, **GARNAULT** (Local Interest) on the south corner of Bulls Cross and Turkey Street. Built in 1860 it was the birthplace of B.J.T. Bosanquet, the Middlesex and England cricketer who invented the "googly" in 1903.

12. In 1724 Michael Garnault purchased Bowling Green House, an Elizabethan mansion at Bulls Cross. This house passed to Henry Carington Bowles when he married Ann Garnault. He demolished the mansion and built **MYDDELTON HOUSE** (Grade II), the Bowles family house from 1818 to 1954. The house is now the headquarters of the Lee Valley Regional Park Authority and is not open to the public but the gardens, reached from the drive with ornate wrought iron gates opposite the junction with Turkey Street, are open daily. (There is an admission charge). This was the lifelong home of the youngest son of H.C.Bowles, E.A. Bowles, a vice-president of the Royal Horticultural Society and a famous plantsman. He created the gardens at Myddelton House, introduced many new plants into cultivation and was regarded as the expert on crocus and other species.

Historic reminders of Enfield's past can be found in the gardens including the stone MARKET CROSS (Grade II) which stood in Enfield Market from 1826 to 1904, the iron bridge (1832) over the old course of the New River and a lake terrace with stone ornaments and balustrades from Old London Bridge.

13. Return to Bulls Cross and on the opposite corner of Turkey Street you will see an attractively proportioned 18th century house, formerly known as Winterton. It has been divided into three homes **THE GATE HOUSE, WEST LODGE AND EAST LODGE** (Grade II)

14. Continue northwards to the hamlet of Bulls Cross. The name is believed to be a corruption of Bedall's Cross, a medieval landmark cross which stood at the junction with Whitewebbs Lane and is mentioned in a document of 1483. The weatherboarded **PIED BULL PUBLIC HOUSE** (Grade II) is 17th century or earlier. The left hand section of the building was once used as the kennels for hunting dogs. Beyond the cottages the road continues along the line of Ermine Street into the Theobolds Estate although a detour is now necessary to cross the M25 motorway.

Capel Manor Stables and former Coachhouse

15. Instead, bear right into Bullsmoor Lane to the entrance of **CAPEL MANOR** (Grade II), built in the 18th century on the site of Honeylands Manor House for Rawson Hart Bodham, a former Governor of Bombay. The last private owner was Col. Sydney Medcalf, a noted horse breeder, The **STABLES AND FORMER COACHHOUSE** (Grade II) are surmounted by a square brick tower with clock face on each side and 1954 weathervane depicting one of the prize-winning Clydesdale carthorses he bred. The house is now the headquarters of Capel Manor College, Greater London's only specialist college of horticulture and countryside studies. The gardens are laid out in a variety of styles and are open daily (admission charge).

From Capel Manor the A10 Cambridge Road, can be seen ahead with buses to many parts of the borough.

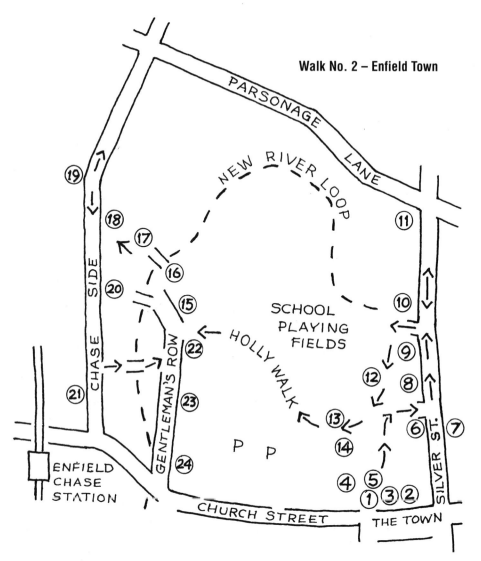

Walk No. 2 – Enfield Town

1. The Market Place	9. No.90 Silver Street	17. New River bridges
2. Old Vestry House	10. Enfield Court	18. Westwood Cottage
3. Barclays Bank	11. Parsonage Lane corner	19. Christ Church
4. King's Head	12. Chapel of Rest	20. Chase Side
5. St. Andrew's Church	13. Uvedale House	21. Chase Green
6. The Vicarage	14. Enfield Grammar School	22. Archway House
7. Church School of Industry	15. Gentleman's Row (north)	23. Gentleman's Row (south)
8. White Lodge	16. River View	24. The Stag

Heritage Walk No. 2
Enfield Town

Enfield developed from a number of scattered hamlets in the Forest of Middlesex. By 1086 the Manor of Enfield was an established estate and included Enfield Chase, a hunting forest of some 8000 acres to the north and west of the village.

1. The walk begins in the **MARKET PLACE**. In 1303 Edward 1 granted the Lord of the Manor the right to hold a weekly market. A new charter, (a copy of which in St. Andrew's Church) was presented to the Parish by James 1 in 1618, giving the people a right to hold a weekly market "for ever". The present Market Place was created in 1632 on the site of a house called "The Vine". The original market house was replaced by the market cross in 1826 and then, in 1904, by the present columned, wooden building. A plaque commemorates the visit of Queen Elizabeth II in 2003 to mark the 800th anniversary of the market.

*Market Place
and St. Andrew's
Parish Church*

2. Although it was in abeyance for many years, the market was revived in the 1870s and flourishes today under the management of the Old Enfield Charitable Trust: their office is in the **THE OLD VESTRY HOUSE** (Grade II) No.22 The Town, just to the east of the Market Place. This small hexagonal building (right) dates from 1829 and was once used as the beadle's office with two lock-up cells.

3. The architect of **BARCLAYS BANK** (right) (surprisingly only listed Local Interest), on the corner of the Market Place was W. Gilbert Scott in 1897. The world's first cashpoint machine was installed here in 1967, an event recorded by a plaque on the front of the building.

4. THE KING'S HEAD public house (Local Interest) was rebuilt in 1899 on the site of an earlier 16th century inn. It has tile-hung upper storeys, half timbered gables, finely detailed doors, carved brackets and etched glass on the ground floor.

5. The entrance to **ST. ANDREW'S PARISH CHURCH** (Grade B) leads directly off the north side of the Market Place. It is an unusually large church by Middlesex standards, consisting of a west tower, a nave with north and south aisles, a south porch and a chancel where a 13th century window can be seen on the south wall. The tower and nave arcades date from the 14th century. The north aisle with the stair turret to the former roof loft dates from about 1500. The south aisle and porch were rebuilt in 1826. Things to note within the church are the organ case of 1752, a large brass memorial dated 1446 to Joyce, Lady Tiptoft and the fine monument to Sir Nicholas Raynton, the first owner of Forty Hall and a Lord Mayor of London.

6. Leave the church by the south porch, turn left across the churchyard, noting several fine 18th and 19th century tombs, towards the eastern path. Ahead is the Parish Centre Gateway erected in memory of a former chairman of Enfield Preservation Society, Major C.A. Lane. Turn left along the path between the churchyard and the high brick wall of the vicarage garden which is faced with some fascinating early carved headstones. Note the tablet above the garden gate and the view through the peepholes. **THE VICARAGE** (Grade II) is basically an L-shaped house, some of which dates from the 15th century. Much of its present appearance, including the Dutch style elevations, results from a drastic re-shaping in 1845 but the earlier form can be discerned from Silver Street.

7. Leave the churchyard through a cast iron gate which, with the railings, was salvaged from Fir Tree House in Silver Street. This house was demolished in 1975 for the building of the Civic Centre. Turn right to Silver Street where facing you is the former **CHURCH SCHOOL OF INDUSTRY** (Local Interest), a charity school built in 1876 to train girls for domestic service. It later became a preparatory school, then a printing works. No. 45 was the Cozy Cinema in 1909 and No. 43 was a Drill Hall for the Enfield Town Company of the 3rd Middlesex Volunteers.

8. Turn left into Silver Street and pass two previously identical HOUSES, Nos. 59 and 60. (Grade II) which date from 1810. Adjoining is **WHITE LODGE** (Grade II), which is thought to be a 17th century house with 18th century weatherboarding. It was once the home of Dr. Jacob Vale Asbury, Charles Lamb's doctor, and from 1862 to 1895 of Joseph Whitaker, founder of Whitaker's Almanacs.

9. No. 90 SILVER STREET (Grade II), an attractive Georgian building, screened by trees, is now used as Council offices. Opposite is the modern Civic Centre, the first stage of which was opened in 1961 and the second part in 1975. Outside it can be seen The Enfield, the heraldic emblem of the borough.

10. Continue up Silver Street past **ENFIELD COURT**, (Grade II) a late 17th/early 18th century building which was once the home of Colonel Sir Alfred Somerset. It has been part of the Grammar School since 1924.

11. Walk to the **CORNER OF PARSONAGE LANE**. It was planted with shrubs by Enfield Preservation Society and there is a plaque commemorating Irene Smith's 26 years' service as Hon. Secretary of Enfield Preservation Society.

12. Retrace your steps briefly down Silver Street to the first path on right beside the bridge over the New River. Then turn left on a footpath skirting school playing fields with glimpses of three church spires: Christ Church. Trinity Church and St. Mary Magdalene. Pass the **CHAPEL OF REST** (Local Interest) which was built originally to house the parish fire engine and later converted into a mortuary.

13. Enter the churchyard again through the iron gateway but now take the diagonal path to the right with **UVEDALE HOUSE AND UVEDALE COTTAGE** (both Grade II) facing you. Uvedale House was originally a Tudor cottage but is much altered externally. Uvedale Cottage wraps round the northern end of the House. Dr. Uvedale was the Headmaster of the Grammar School from 1664-76 and achieved fame as a horticulturist. He introduced the Sweet Pea and other plants and trees into England.

14. Make a short detour down Church Walk from the front of Uvedale House to view the oldest (c.1590) part of **ENFIELD GRAMMAR SCHOOL** (Grade II*), founded in 1557. This Tudor building is of red brick with mullioned dormer windows set into the elaborately gabled tiled roof. The lower stone framed windows were inserted in Victorian times.

Enfield Grammar School

15. Return to Uvedale House and turn left into Holly Walk passing newer parts of the Grammar School on the left and Enfield County School

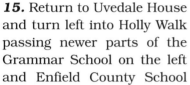

on the right: a good example of Middlesex County Council school architecture. Continue along Holly Walk until it joins Gentleman's Row. Turn right past **Nos. 27-33 GENTLEMAN'S ROW** (Grade II) – a row of early 19th century cottages set in pairs with a blocked window between each pair to maintain the symmetry. On the opposite side of the road **RIVULET HOUSE** (grade II) is a compact 19th century brick villa with a Georgian façade. Note the three round arched stable doors of **BRECON HOUSE** (Grade II) on the end wall.before crossing the bridge over the New River Loop to see the front of this impressive mid 18th century house of three storeys with single storey flanking blocks each with a Venetian window.

16. Next door in River View is **THE LAURELS** (Grade II) a 17th century timber-framed house which was re-fronted with stucco and parapet in the early 19th century. Adjacent is **THE CROWN AND HORSESHOES** (Grade II). There has been an inn here since

1716 but the present building was constructed in the 19th century. It was a favourite watering hole of Charles Lamb, the essayist, when he lived in the area.

17. Note **THE CAST IRON BRIDGE** (Grade II) beside this public house: it is one of four on this stretch of the New River which are all listed and date from early to mid-19th century.

18. Walk briefly down Horseshoe Lane, opposite the Crown and Horseshoes and then turn first right into Chase Side, noting at No.5 the fine rubbed brickwork. Continue up Chase Side past two houses successively occupied by Charles Lamb and his sister, Mary. Both No. 89 **WESTWOOD COTTAGE**, (Grade II) and No. 87 commemorate this with plaques although, unfortunately, the 19th century front of the latter has been sadly desecrated and much altered in the 1930s.

19. On the opposite side of the road can be seen **CHRIST CHURCH**, (Grade II). Now a United Reformed church it was built for Congregationalists in the Gothic Revival manner with an elegant tall spire in 1874.

20. Turn back down **CHASE SIDE** towards The Town. The following buildings are of interest and all are listed Grade II:
No.103 – early to mid-18th century two storey house
Nos. 93-99 – 17th/19th century houses
No. 85 – two storey weatherboarded 18th century cottage
Nos. 81-83 – built by Mr. Nott in the 18th century for his two daughters, Hannah and Lizzie, with a central passage closed by a third door
No. 79 – yellow brick 19th century house
No. 77 – early to mid 19th century villa of stock brick with parapet
Nos. 22-36 – Gloucester Place Cottages, a terrace of eight houses built in 1823 for artisans.
The Moon Under Water is unlisted but is of interest as it has been

a public house only since 1988. It had previously been used as a primary school (1838-1901), a milk depot and a restaurant.

21. CHASE GREEN, on the right is a small remnant of Enfield Chase, a favourite hunting ground of Henry VIII, Elizabeth I and James I. There is a tradition, which awaits proof, that victims of the Great Plague are buried here. A row of houses known as The Limes covers the site of the pond and post house, which was demolished in 1911. In 1935 there was a proposal to erect a town hall on Chase Green but it was bitterly opposed by prominent citizens who following their successful campaign founded the Enfield Preservation Society in 1936.

22. Turn left on to the path between the end house of Chase Side and the Gardens and cross the New River by another of the listed bridges. To the right will be seen the water sculpture, which commemorates the millennium and the restoration of the New River Loop. There are attractive views with the spire of Trinity Church to the right. Bear left, passing a pleasant group of old houses facing the green and stop at **ARCHWAY HOUSE** (Grade II) No. 23 Gentleman's Row. This elegant building (1750) was a tavern from 1835-1914 with an orchard, garden and skittle alley An arched carriageway, from which the house derives its name, leads to Chapel Street (formerly Love's Row).

23. From Archway House continue down **GENTLEMAN'S ROW** with the houses on your left. Their gardens on the right, separated by the footpath, were obtained by successive incursions into Enfield Chase. These plots were sold to the occupants in 1777 when Enfield Chase was sold off by the parish. Many of the houses were brick clad in the 18th century disguising much earlier timber framed origins. Most display a bronze Listed Building Plaque which are produced by Enfield Preservation Society. The following are all Grade II except where noted:
No. 21 Sedgecombe, a 17th century timber-framed house with

an early 18th century dark red brick front. The fine doorcase of fluted pilasters and entablature is particularly notable.

No. 19 Eastbury is similar to its neighbour.

No. 17 Clarendon Cottage (Grade II*) was originally a 16th century hall house of two bays, an extension being added in the 17th century. A wooden plaque notes its association with Charles and Mary Lamb who stayed on two occasions in 1825 and 1827 when it was a boarding house.

Nos. 13-15 Fortescue Villas were built on the site of the ancient Fortescue Hall: these two large houses are now divided into flats. The 19th century cast iron railings with ball and spike finials are also listed. The Coach House, an L-shaped timber frame building of upper cruck construction was originally a barn.and converted to a house in the 1950s.

No. 11 Fortescue Lodge, this late 17th century stableman's cottage for Fortescue Hall.was converted to a house in 1710 and given a Georgian style facade.

Nos. 7 and 9 Elm House is 17th century with 18th century additions: this house has served as a school, a Girl Guide Hall, a store for antique furniture and a convalescent home for wounded soldiers in World War 1. The southern extension has been split off to form No. 7.

No.5 Little Park is ostensibly a large Edwardian house which has been substantially altered but it has parts dating back to Tudor times. An extension, known as the Tudor Room, was built to house a superb stone fireplace bearing the royal arms, the crowned Tudor rose, the crowned portcullis, and the initials E.R. There is also some fine panelling and the inscription in Latin: The favour of the King is like dew upon the grass. These historic pieces were removed from the nearby Enfield Palace, an old

manor house, on its demolition in 1927.

No.1 The Public Offices (Grade II) – this imposing Georgian building was once a magnificent private house with a large garden and lake to the rear. Bought in 1888 by the Enfield Board of Health it has served many purposes including the district's first public library. It currently houses the Registrar and other borough departments.

The Public Offices

24. On the corner **THE STAG** public house was constructed in 1897 on the site of an older inn. Cross to the bus stands and turn left into The Town to return to the Market Place.

Walk No. 3 – Edmonton

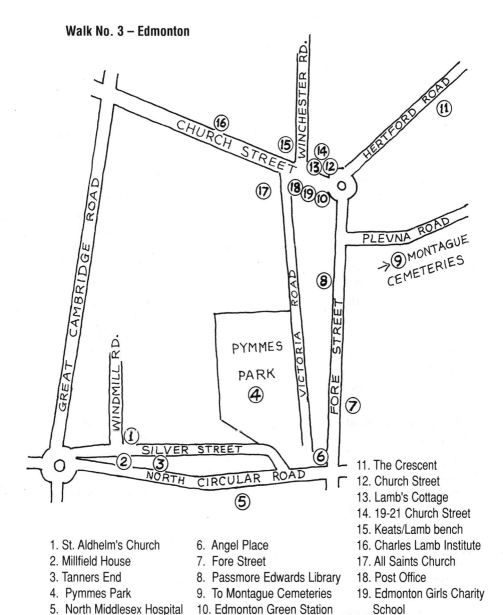

11. The Crescent
12. Church Street
13. Lamb's Cottage
14. 19-21 Church Street
15. Keats/Lamb bench
16. Charles Lamb Institute
17. All Saints Church
18. Post Office
19. Edmonton Girls Charity
    School

1. St. Aldhelm's Church
2. Millfield House
3. Tanners End
4. Pymmes Park
5. North Middlesex Hospital
6. Angel Place
7. Fore Street
8. Passmore Edwards Library
9. To Montague Cemeteries
10. Edmonton Green Station

Heritage Walk No. 3
Edmonton

Edmonton was originally two separate settlements, Lower and Upper, and the gap between them was not finally closed until c.1870. It remained a relatively rural area, cut off from London, until 1849 when a station opened at Edmonton Green on the branch from Angel Road to Enfield Town. The direct line to Enfield Town, serving Silver Street and the present Edmonton Green Station, opened in 1872. The original low-level station was used for some rush hour workmen's trains until 1939 and the line survived for freight traffic until 1964: the station buildings were demolished in 1970. The railways offered easy access to London and cheap workmen's fares so the district became a working class residential area, attracting many from the East End. The original hamlet of Upper Edmonton was sited at the junction of the present Fore Street, Silver Street and Angel Road. Lower Edmonton was the administrative and religious centre of the parish and developed around Church Street, with the ancient church of All Saints and Edmonton Green

1. Begin the walk at the gates of Millfield House and Weir Hall Library in Silver Street, (near the junction of the Great Cambridge and North Circular roads). Opposite you will see **ST. ALDHELM'S CHURCH** (Grade C). which was built in 1903. The architect was William Douglas Caroe who interpreted the building in the Gothic style with Arts and Craft influence.

2. Go through the gates by the 19th century **ENTRANCE LODGE** (Grade II) to **MILLFIELD HOUSE** (Grade II*) which was built in 1796 as a country house. From 1849-1913 it was used by the Strand Board of Guardians as a workhouse school and then housed Belgian refugees during World War 1. It is linked at the back to buildings

Millfield House

added from 1917 when it was converted into St. David's Hospital. It has been an arts centre since 1971. It contains an impressive staircase. Also listed are the 18th century brick boundary walls.

3. Walk in front of the House and take the sign posted Pymmes Brook Trail left. Less than 150 years ago this brook flowed through a rural area rich in plant and animal life. This changed when the railways, industry and urbanisation arrived but today's Trail allows walkers to enjoy a green corridor for 10 miles between Monken Hadley and Edmonton. In **TANNERS END**, once the centre of the local leather industry, there are two Victorian chapels. Gladys Aylward, whose life as a missionary in China was told in the film "Inn of the Sixth Happiness", used to worship here. In Elizabethan times Silver Street widened out here into a large green which stretched from the present junction with Victoria Road.

4. Enter **PYMMES PARK** and bear right towards the walled garden. There are viewing panels in the walls if it is not open. This is Edmonton's oldest park, opened to the public in 1897. During the 16th century the Pymmes estate was owned by the powerful Robert Cecil, later the Earl of Salisbury and Chief Minister of Queen Elizabeth 1 and King James 1. It remained in the owner-ship of the Cecil family until the 18th century. The Ray family owned it in the 19th century and the Nawab of Bengal was in exile here after a dispute with Queen Victoria's government. Pymmes House was destroyed by fire in 1940. The GARDEN WALLS (Grade II) and the walled garden are all that survive from the Tudor period.

5. Note the **NORTH MIDDLESEX HOSPITAl** on the opposite side of the North Circular Road. Its buildings incorporate part of the former Edmonton Workhouse which was built in 1842 to house the poor of six parishes

6. Continue ahead to the east side to leave the park, turn right towards the North Circular and then bear left through a small grassy area beside Silver Street station. Continue to the junction of Fore Street and the North Circular Road. On the left is **ANGEL PLACE** (Grade II GV), Nos. 183-195 Fore Street. This mid-18th century terrace dates from about 1780 and retains many original features such as the doorcases, mansard roofs and dormer windows. A blue plaque on the flank wall of No. 183 commemorates the Angel Public House, demolished for road widening in 1968, where the Stamford Hill Green Lanes Turnpike Trust met from 1713-1826.

7. Continue up **FORE STREET** and note on the opposite side of the road Nos. 236 and 238 (Grade II) listed because of the Georgian features they have kept such as the original railings and Doric door surrounds. Nos. 258 and 260 (Grade II) are listed for similar reasons. **No. 320, THE OLD POLICE STATION** (Grade II) has now been sympathetically converted into apartments.

The Old Police Station

29

*The former
Passmore
Library*

8. On the opposite side of Fore Street the impressive former **PASSMORE EDWARDS LIBRARY** (Grade II) was built in 1897 to the design of Maurice B. Adams and housed the Edmonton library until 1991. It is currently used as a Sikh community centre.

9. On the opposite side of the main road, Plevna Road leads you to the **MONTAGUE CEMETERIES**. The Tottenham Park and Jewish Cemeteries were designated as a second conservation area in 1996 because of their unique landscape qualities. Both contain fine monuments. However as this site measures 14.8 hectares, it is suggested that you do not include this area in your walk but visit it on another day.

10. Continue along Fore Street to **EDMONTON GREEN STATION** (called Lower Edmonton until 1992) which was opened by the Great Eastern Railway in 1872 as part of its direct line to Enfield via Bethnal Green and Hackney Downs. At platform level it retains the original canopies with the ridge and furrow roof, characteristic of Great Eastern suburban stations of that period. (These are partly visible from the corner of Church Street if you do not wish to climb the stairs to the platforms)

The Crescent

11. Cross to Edmonton Green shopping centre, currently (2006) being re-built on what was once a village green and walk ahead to Hertford Road. **THE CRESCENT** (Grade II GV), Nos. 84-132 Hertford Road forms an impressive terrace built in the mid 1820s and is a reflection of the wealth and social pretensions of 19th century Edmonton. Further houses were added at both ends and the pediment is off centre. In front of the house there were, originally, two porters lodges and a grand carriage drive.

12. Cross Hertford Road and turn back towards the station but bear right into **CHURCH STREET**, the heart of the ancient parish of Edmonton. It was the first conservation area in Edmonton, created in 1970 because of its ancient church and churchyard. Note the plaque to the poet, John Keats, over the pharmacy on right.

13. The first building to note is no.11. **LAMB'S COTTAGE** (Grade II*) (right) a timber framed cottage of two storeys

31

and an attic with a slated mansard roof. The front and interior remain much as remodelled in the 18th century with Georgian panelling, arches and open-string staircase. (This private house is usually open during Open House London weekend). Originally known as Bay Tree or Walden's Cottage, it was a private mental home in the 19th century and later a Vestry Office. It was renamed after its most famous resident, the essayist Charles Lamb, chose to join his sister, Mary, a patient, in 1833. He died the following year.

14. Nearby, **19 and 21 CHURCH STREET** (Grade II) are a fine pair of Georgian houses with slated mansard roofs and attics.

15. A **CARVED STONE BENCH** on the corner of Winchester Road commemorates Charles Lamb and John Keats, both former residents of Church Street. This was the original site of the fire station, now rebuilt further along the street.

16. THE CHARLES LAMB INSITUTE (Grade II) is a stone-faced building in the style of a Tudor college. It was built in 1908 and is currently used as the Tower Gym.

17. Cross the road to **CHURCH OF ALL SAINTS** (Grade B), the ancient parish church of Edmonton. Although mainly 15th century, incorporated into the west wall is a fragment of 12th century masonry of the earliest church on this site. Monuments date from 16th to 19th centuries.and Charles and Mary Lamb are buried in the churchyard.

18. Turn back down Church Street towards Edmonton Green on the same side as the church to Nos. 44-48, **THE POST OFFICE SORTING OFFICE** (Local Interest). It was built in the early 20th century and the forecourt wall and railings are also listed.

19. Further down the road you will come to **EDMONTON GIRLS CHARITY SCHOOL** and the adjacent **SCHOOLMISTRESS'S**

All Saints Church

HOUSE (Grade II GV). The school was established by public subscription in 1778 on similar lines to the Bluecoat schools and above the door can be seen a statue of a girl in school uniform holding an open book. The school closed in 1904 and the building is now a public hall. The adjoining **TERRACE** (nos. 20, 20A, 22 and 22A) (Grade II GV) are 18th century cottages, the frontages of which were converted into shops in 19th century.

From Edmonton Green there are trains and buses to Silver Street, Bush Hill Park, Enfield Town and other parts of the borough.

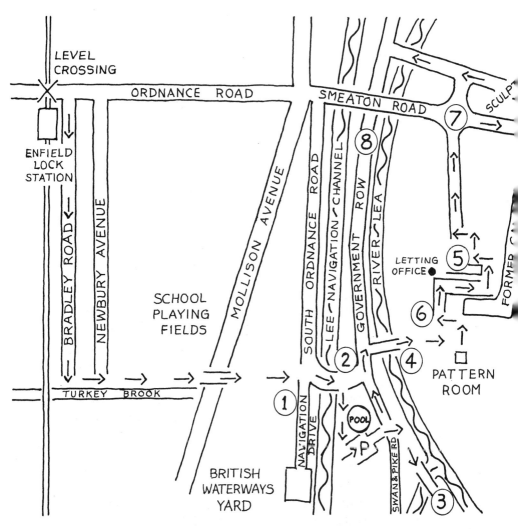

Walk No. 4 – Enfield Lock

1. Lea House
2. Lock House
3. King George Pumping Station
4. Royal Small Arms Factory
5. Machine shop
6. Factory Manager's office
7. Water Tower
8. Government Row

Heritage Walk No. 4
Enfield Lock

The area known as Enfield Lock developed with the expansion of the Royal Small Arms Factory in 1854 when it formed a self-contained community with its own housing, school, church, police station and hotel. It was designated as a conservation area in 1976 (but the RSAF site itself was excluded) and it forms an important part of Enfield's industrial history. The RSAF closed in 1988 and the island site has been developed for housing but several of the original buildings can still be seen.

1. Start at Enfield Lock Railway Station, turn right and almost immediately right again into Bradley Road.. Continue to the end of this road and turn left at the bridge. (The first part of this walk is along the route of section 18 of the London Loop). Take the path to the left of Turkey Brook, cross Newbury Avenue and continue beside the Brook, past school playing fields on your left and take the right hand fork to cross the bridge over Mollison Avenue, (the North-South Road). Follow the path ahead until you come to some bollards and turn right into Navigation Drive. **LEA HOUSE**, on the right, is now boarded up but was built in 1792 for the Surveyor to the Trustees of the River Lea Navigation. If the gate ahead is open, go into the BRITISH WATERWAYS YARD. There is an office in the building with Lee Conservancy over the door where maps and information on the area are available, Walnut trees were planted round the central grass island to provide wood for rifle stocks and there are several old buildings in the yard.

2. Leave by the same gate and return to the end of Navigation Drive. Cross the bridge to the right for a view of the lock. **LOCK HOUSE AND LOCK COTTAGE** (Local Interest) are examples of

Lock House and Lock Cottage

19th century canal architecture. Turn right immediately at end of bridge and follow the metal handrails to Swan and Pike Pool which is reputed to be home to a legendary pike and to be five metres deep. If you could not gain access to the British Waterways Yard, the buildings and trees can now be seen on the opposite bank.

3. Walk through the small car park on the left to the road and cross to the Sewardstone footpath sign ahead. Go along the footpath to the second bridge to view **WATER TOWER HOUSE, PUMP HOUSE AND RETORT HOUSE, KING GEORGE PUMPING STATION** (Grade IIGV) There is no public access to these buildings except sometimes during the Open House London weekend in September. Water Tower House, opened in 1913 by the Metropolitan Water Board, is an imposing building in Edwardian baroque style. The Pump House has corner turrets and once housed five cast iron gas pumps in deep brick-lined pits in a unique design, the first example of its type in the world. Each pump was capable of raising 40 million gallons of water daily into

Pumping Station

the King George Reservoir. Retort House was used until 1968 for storing gas made from anthracite before it was passed to the Pump Room.

4. Leave the London Loop here and retrace your steps along the footpath to Swan and Pike Road, and turn right past the Mill House and the former Royal Small Arms Tavern. This public house dated from 1858 and was owned by the RSAF. It closed in 1981 but re-opened as a restaurant called Rifles in 1986. At present (2007) it seems probable that the building will be demolished and replaced by housing. Go straight ahead into Government Row for a few yards and then turn right opposite the back of Lock Cottage to a footbridge for access into the former **ROYAL SMALL ARMS FACTORY**. The Royal Armoury Mills (later RSAF) opened at Enfield Lock in 1816 and swords and bayonets were made as well as guns and musket barrels. The factory supplied the Enfield Pattern 1853 rifle to the armies of both North and South during the American Civil War. The famous Lee-Enfield Magazine rifle MK1 was first produced in 1895. During World War I women were employed for the first time at the factory. Large numbers of weapons, such as Bren and Sten guns were produced during World War II. The war in Korea in 1950 also resulted in largescale manufacture but the factory closed in

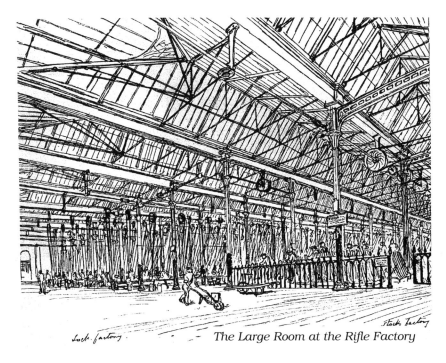

The Large Room at the Rifle Factory

1988. The site was subsequently developed for housing although a few of the original buildings have been preserved.

5. The first building across the bridge is the former Police Station because this was the main factory gate and tight security was necessary. Continue ahead to the second building on the right, the former PATTERN ROOM where "the sealed patterns", the standards by which all British manufactured small arms were judged, were kept. Go through the arches opposite the Pattern Room and facing you will be the front of a large building with a clock tower. This is the **MACHINE SHOP** (Grade II) with attached range, completed in 1856 to accommodate machinery from America so that mass production could begin. The bell, called Albert, was cast specifically for this building. The water feature, however, on the site of the former mill head and barge turning pool, is new.

Machine Shop

6. Turn left in front of the arches and ahead you will see the **FACTORY MANAGER'S OFFICE**, the railings of which are listed Grade II. Walk towards the clock tower under which is a small Interpretation Centre with information on the history of RSAF. (For access apply at the Letting and Management Office, on the left hand corner of the main building. It is usually open only Monday-Friday from 10 a.m to 2 p.m). Walk past the clock tower and turn left along the side of the machine shop (now used as a gym), then left twice more and right to bring to the rear of the Machine Shop and the Interpretation Centre, In the passage opposite are some information panels. (A café beside this passage is at present open every day except Sunday. In it can be seen some of the supporting columns which double as drainpipes). If the gate beyond the information panels is open, go through them into the courtyard where you will see an old font, all that remains of the factory church. Leave by gate beyond the font and turn left. (If the courtyard gate is closed, turn left outside café and immediately left again, noting the north light roof designed to capture maximum daylight and the dual purpose columns as seen in the café. Through the gate on the left with sign Courtyard 10-26 you can see the font).

7. Walk straight ahead, through a car park by the shop and some new housing to the **WATER TOWER** which provided the factory with water for services but not for drinking as it was pumped from the River Lee to the tank at the top. Turn right along the road to the north end of the water feature where there is a small square with seats. Look to the left and you will see a sculpture incorporating six cast iron columns from the machine shop. After viewing this, turn left opposite the sculpture and go along a road of new houses straight to a bridge over the River Lea.

Government Row

8. After crossing the river, turn left on the path by the Lee Navigation Canal along **GOVERNMENT ROW** which was built in 1854 to house workers from the RSAF. Continue under the main bridge to the island to note Nos. 4-14, 18-28 (Grade II GV) and Nos. 30-31 (Local Interest). Then turn back to the bridge steps to climb to the road above. There are views of Rammey March, owned by the Lea Valley Regional Park Authority and a designated Site of Scientific Interest.

In front of you is Ordnance Road where Enfield Lock Station is situated and there is a bus stop for routes 121 and 491 on the bridge.

Heritage Walk No. 5
Southgate

Southgate came into being as a result of the creation in about 1200 of Enfield Chase, the village being centred upon the south gate of this royal hunting ground. Whilst local peasants had the right to graze animals upon the Chase, the woodlands of Southgate were far more extensively exploited, producing timber for building and fuel, bark for the tanners of Enfield and Edmonton and charcoal, the latter industry surviving into the early 19th century. By this time Southgate had become the home of some wealthy estate owners as well as arable farmers, though signs of the impending urbanisation of the 20th century were even then at hand. By 1851, with the opening of a station at Colney Hatch (later re-named New Southgate) on the Great Northern Railway, the construction of New Southgate housing estates was beginning, though the Walker family of Arnos Grove stopped the development spreading north of Bowes Road and extensive house building did not begin in Southgate until the early 1900s. The opening of the Piccadilly Line Underground extension in 1932/33 encouraged further largescale housing development and soon the transformation of Southgate into a residential suburb was complete.

1. No more appropriate spot could be chosen to start this walk than the site of the south gate itself which stood at the **SOUTHGATE CIRCUS END** of what is now **CHASE ROAD**.

2. Across the busy Circus is **SOUTHGATE UNDERGROUND STATION** (Grade II) and accompanying parade of shops. Its striking design, making it the hub of the Circus, came from the architectural practice of Charles Holden. Four of his local stations (Arnos Grove, Cockfosters, Oakwood and this one) are listed as

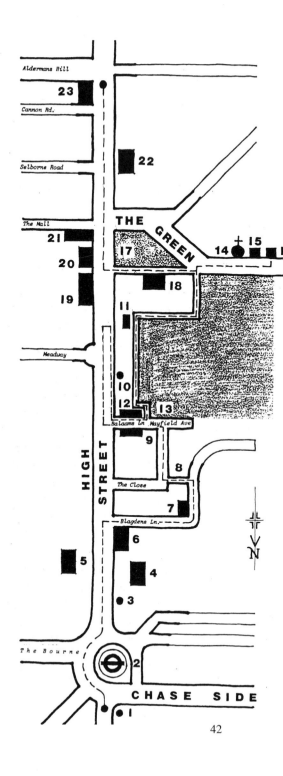

Walk No. 5 –
Southgate

1. Southgate Circus
2. Underground station
3. No. 151 High Street
4. Southgate College
5. Southgate House
6. Georgian Houses
7. Minchenden Lodge
8. Bladgens Close
9. Cottages, Balaams Lane
10. Site of Eagle Hall
11. Ellington Court
12. Baird Memorial Homes
13. Walker Cricket Ground
14. Christ Church
15. Site of Weld Chapel
16. Minchenden Oak
17. Southgate Green
18. Nos. 2-5 The Green
19. Nos. 40-41 and 38-39 The Green
20. Georgian Cottages (nos. 23 32)
21. The Olde Cherry Tree Inn
22. Arnos Grove, now Beaumont Care Centre
23. The Hermitage and Nos. 4-6A Cannon Hill

buildings of special architectural importance. Before the coming of the Tube the Circus was a collection of old buildings called Bunker's Corner, named after a firm of wheelwrights situated here.

3. Turn right outside the station and go down the High Street. On the right hand side a **PLAQUE ON NO. 151** marks the site of the village hall which in 1882 housed the early meetings of the Southgate Local Board of Health, predecessor of Southgate Urban District Council. The road opposite is named after John Bradshaw who lived at the Grange (now demolished) and was a great benefactor of Southgate.

4. Further along the High Street on the right-hand side stands **SOUTHGATE COLLEGE** built in 1963 on sites once occupied by the nursery and market gardens of seedsmen R & G Cuthbert and by the Wilderness, one of Southgate's larger houses.

5. Immediately opposite, behind a high wall and surrounded by many fine old trees, is **SOUTHGATE HOUSE** (Grade II*) a building of yellow brick with stone dressings and a curved porch, dating from about 1780. A plaque near the front door records its occupation by Baron Lawrence (who relieved the siege of Delhi) from 1861 until his appointment as the first Governor-General of India in 1864. It was then owned by the Walker family until 1922 when it was sold to Middlesex County Council and housed Minchenden School from 1924 to 1987. It is now part of Southgate College.

6. Opposite the boundary wall of Southgate House is a row of fine **GEORGIAN HOUSES**. Nos. 111-117 (Croft Cottage, Holcombe House, Avington and Avington Cottage) are listed IIGV. During the 19th century No. 107 (Grade 11 GV with No.109) became the Zion House Academy, kept by Robert Blagden, a land surveyor who gave his name to Blagdens Lane.

Georgian Houses at 111-117, High Street

PETER A.J.B

7. The walk now turns right down Blagdens Lane at the end of which stands **MINCHENDEN LODGE** (Local Interest). It was once owned by the landlord of the Cherry Tree Inn on Southgate Green. There is an unproven story that Queen Victoria and Prince Albert stayed at the Lodge one night after they had officially opened Colney Hatch Asylum. It is now used as a centre for the elderly.

8. Continue down **BLAGDENS CLOSE** through an area of late 20th century housing to a footpath on the left between The Lodge (No.3A) and No 3B which leads to the Close, a development of the 1930s in which several mature trees were allowed to remain.

9. Turn right down the Close and then left along Mayfield Avenue, named after a large house that stood nearby. Mayfield Avenue leads into Balaams Lane. Near the end on the left is a row of **COTTAGES** originally built in 1792 and rebuilt in 1911 – the clapboarding is a more recent addition.

10. At the end of Balaams Lane make a short detour right along the High Street to see the site of **EAGLE HALL**, opposite the Woolpack public house. Eagle Hall, demolished after bomb damage in 1940, was the birthplace in 1784 of James Leigh Hunt, poet and essayist, as recorded on a blue plaque fixed to the wall of the modern residential development between the two shop fronts.

11. The detour continues a little further along the High Street to visit **ELLINGTON COURT**, a block of flats standing well back from the road, on the right-hand side. This was designed by the eminent 20th century architect Sir Frederick Gibberd in 1936.

12. Retrace your steps and turn left into Balaams Lane. On the left are the **BAIRD MEMORIAL HOMES** (1894) named after the first vicar of Christ Church. A more modern wing, in keeping with the original building, has been added. There is an explanatory plaque on the front facing the church across the field.

13. Next to the Baird Memorial Homes is the entrance to a footpath round part of the **WALKER CRICKET GROUND**. This land, formerly Chapel Fields, was purchased by Isaac Walker from the third Duke of Chandos in 1853 to enlarge his estate and his son John laid out the land for cricket soon afterwards. He was the eldest of seven brothers, none of whom ever married, and he made this one of the principal cricket grounds in the country. Several of the brothers played for England and in 1858 10,000 people saw the Sixteen of Southgate beat United All England on this ground. Continue on the footpath to the car park opposite Christ Church.

14. CHRIST CHURCH (Grade II*) was built in 1863. It was designed by Sir George Gilbert Scott and contains windows of Pre-Raphaelite stained glass supplied by William Morris & Co. to designs by Rossetti and Burne-Jones. Part of the church boundary wall is 17th century. In this wall, at the east end, is a small door, presumably a private entrance for the family at nearby Arnolds.

Christ Church

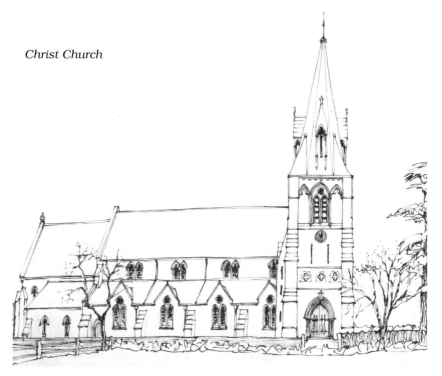

15. In the churchyard at the west end of the church is the site of the **WELD CHAPEL**. This was built in 1615 by Sir John Weld who lived at Arnolds and it was replaced by the present church. The Weld family moved to Lulworth, Dorset, and became Roman Catholics.

16. Adjoining the churchyard and reached through a gate in the wall is the memorial garden containing the **MINCHENDEN OAK**. This tree, a survivor of the ancient Forest of Middlesex, is reputed to be at least 800 years old.

17. Leave the church and walk right to **SOUTHGATE GREEN**, the centre of the Conservation Area which was the hub of the hamlet of South Street in years gone by and included a large pond and stocks. In 1928 the pond was filled in but a pair of stocks (not the original) remains. Close by is a horse trough erected by the Metropolitan Drinking Fountain and Cattle Trough Association.

*Arnoside and
Essex House*

18. Cross to the north side of the Green, which contains a mixture of 18th century and modern buildings, the Parish Centre being an example of how well the new can blend with the old. **No. 2 (OLD HOUSE)**, and **No. 3 (ESSEX COACH HOUSE)** (Grade II GV), **No. 4 (ESSEX HOUSE)** and **No. 5 (ARNOSIDE HOUSE)** (Grade II*GV), and **ARNOSIDE COTTAGE** (Grade IIGV), are characteristic of the 18th century from which they date. The bell on the roof of Arnoside is a reminder that it was once used as a school.

19. Cross the main road to the east side of the Green which also contains some interesting properties: **Nos. 41 (INGLESIDE)** and **40 (ASH LODGE)** (Local Interest) are 19th century houses. The latter was used as the first office of the Southgate Local Board of Health in 1881, as recorded on the plaque. **Nos. 39 (NORBURY HOUSE)** and **38 (SANDFORD HOUSE)** (Grade 11) are late 18th century with a more recent addition to the former. Next to them is a school, formerly a bank, which replaced the house in which the Reverend Benjamin Waugh, founder of the NSPCC, once lived.

20. The row of **GEORGIAN COTTAGES (Nos. 23-32)** (Grade II) next to the school was designed by Michael Searles, architect of the Paragon at Blackheath, and built in the late 18th century. A plaque records their reconstruction with the help of Southgate Civic Trust in 1981. This work included the removal of the shop fronts which had been a feature of the cottages for many years.

21. On the corner of the High Street and The Mall is **THE OLDE CHERRY TREE INN** (Grade II) one of the oldest buildings in Southgate. There was an inn or public house on the land when it was given by Valentine Poole for the benefit of the poor of Barnet in 1624 and the Charity Trust has a record of the Cherry Tree back to 1721. The buttresses and porch were added in 1923 to prevent the walls bulging any further. Two recesses with holes in the ceiling can be seen on the left-hand side of the archway entrance to the inn yard. These were to allow the long coach poles to be stored for the night after coaches had been unloaded and unhorsed.

22. Across Cannon Hill an avenue of red chestnut trees leads to a house originally called ARNOS GROVE and now the **SOUTHGATE BEAUMONT RESIDENTIAL CARE CENTRE** (Grade II*). The centre portion is from the house built in 1723 for James Colebrooke and purchased by Isaac Walker in 1777. The Walker family, which included the seven cricketing brothers, retained possession of it for 141 years. The two wings were added after the building was sold for offices to the North Metropolitan Electric Power Supply Company in 1928. The walls and ceilings of the entrance hall in the mansion have some fine murals depicting the triumphs of Julius Caesar and painted by Gerard Lanscroon when the house was built. (These may be viewed by prior arrangement and sometimes during Open House London weekend). The electric lamp standards in the drive came from the Wembley Exhibition of 1924.

23. Further down Cannon Hill on the opposite side are three houses representing 18th century Southgate and now adapted to modern requirements. **Nos. 6 and 6A** (Grade II), originally known as Cannon House, is now used as a social club by

*Arnos Grove,
now Beaumont Care Centre.*

4 Cannon Hill

The Hermitage

St. Monica's Church, Palmers Green.   The timber built house
next door, **No. 4** (Grade II), was originally the stables and coach
house of Cannon House. **THE HERMITAGE** (Grade 1I) is one of
the few thatched houses remaining in London.

The walk ends here at the corner of Cannon Hill and Alderman's
IIill, opposite Broomfield Park, where buses can be caught to
Enfield, Southgate and other parts of the Borough.

Heritage Walk No. 6
Winchmore Hill

Before the 17th century Winchmore Hill was part of an extensive area of woodland on the edge of Enfield Chase, the remains of what was once a great forest. Inhabited by charcoal burners and woodmen (and a haunt of witches) it was remote from civilisation. In the 17th century it was still considered secluded enough to serve as a refuge for Quakers who were finding it difficult to meet in more populous areas. The 18th and early 19th centuries saw the enclosure and clearing of the woodlands of Enfield Chase and thereafter Winchmore Hill developed into a village community. The Great Northern Railway came to the area in 1871 with its branch line to Enfield when Winchmore Hill Station, the frontage of which has changed little apart from the loss of its west wing, was opened. The area was a rural backwater and Station Road (then known as Middle Lane) was a quiet byway linking the village with the main road to Enfield. The railway, no doubt, accelerated the transition in the 20th century into a suburb of London. Although the old village has been swallowed up by the growth of London, some traces of its former character remain and these have been safeguarded by the establishment of two Conservation Areas.

1. The walk begins at Winchmore Hill Station. Turn right and on your left is The Green, the old centre of Winchmore Hill which still retains some of its village atmosphere. At one time the grassed area was larger and included a pond and a pump. Cross The Green diagonally to No. 212 Hoppers Road, **THE OLD BAKERY** (Grade II) on the left-hand side. This 18th century building retains its original shop front although it has been converted into a private dwelling. The fluted wooden columns have been restored. The early 19th century bread ovens were still in use when it ceased to be a bakery in the 1960s.

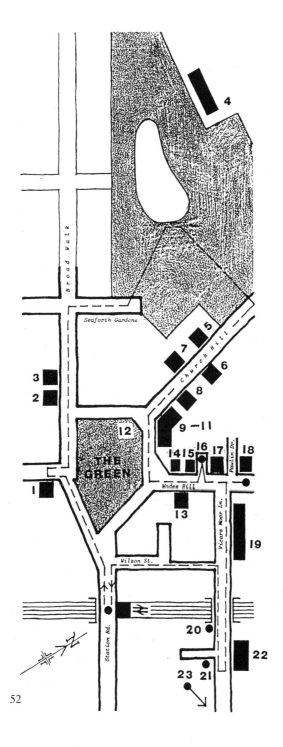

Walk No. 6 –
Winchmore Hill

1. The Old Bakery
2. Cottage, Broad Walk
3. Rowantree House
4. Grovelands House
5. Woodside Cottages
6. Stone Hall Lodge
7. St. Paul's Church
8. Friends Meeting House
9. Devon House
10. Former Village Fire Station
11. King's Head
12. Horse trough on The Green
13. Nos. 17-29 Wades Hill
14. Manhole covers
15. Glenwood House
16. Harwood's Yard
17. Site of Broadfields
18. Esther Doe Lodge
19. Vicars Moor Lane
20. Engraved stone (on bridge)
21. Engraved stone (on site of Roseneath)
22. Nos. 66-76 Vicars Moor Lane
23. Site of Rose Cottage

The Old Bakery

2. Cross Hoppers Road and return towards The Green and turn first left into Broad Walk. The old **COTTAGE .WITH A SHOP FRONTAGE** near the beginning of this road was extended for use as a shop in about 1840. For many years it was used as a drapers. The premises have been extended to the rear in more recent times.

3. Beyond this shop is **ROWANTREE HOUSE/WOODSIDE HOUSE** (Grade II) built during the first half of the 18th century and now divided into two properties. Broad Walk, which follows the line of the old path through Winchmore Hill Wood (formerly Lord's Grove) to Southgate, is a broad tree-lined thoroughfare of spacious houses. Take the second turning on the right, Seaforth Gardens, and then about half way down this road on the left-hand side, a gated path into Grovelands Park. The Grovelands Estate, originally owned by Walker Gray, later became the property of John Donnithorne Taylor, a prominent landowner connected with the Taylor Walker brewery. It remained in his

Rowantree and Woodside House

family until offered for sale early in the 20th century. Some of its land was built on but a large portion was purchased by the Southgate Urban District Council in 1911 as a public park – a farsighted action for which local residents must ever be grateful. Although adapted for public use, the park still retains some of the character of a private estate.

4. On entering the park from Seaforth Gardens take a diagonal path through the woods between the rear garden walls of Broad Walk to your left and a stream. This is all the woodland that remains of the once extensive Winchmore Hill Wood, vividly recalled by Henrietta Cresswell in *Winchmore Hill: Memories of a Lost Village.* You will then come to a path bordering Grovelands Lake, from where there is a good view of **GROVELANDS HOUSE** (Grade I), originally Southgate Grove. It was built for Walker Gray in 1797 to a design by John Nash and is considered to be one of his finest classical mansions. The park was landscaped by Humphry Repton at the same time. This was the first major

Grovelands House

commission undertaken jointly by Nash and Repton when they were in partnership. The house passed to John Donnithorne Taylor with the rest of the estate in 1840 and it was finally sold for use as a military hospital in the First World War. It later served as a convalescent home for the Royal Northern and local hospitals until 1977. For several years it was unoccupied but is now, with new extensions, a private psychiatric hospital called Grovelands Priory. By the railings in front of the house is a ha-ha or ditch, built to prevent the herd of red deer which once inhabited the park from straying into the gardens. (It is usually possible to view some of the interior, including the delightful octagonal Birdcage Room, during Open House London weekend in September).

5. Turn right alongside the lake briefly and at the first corner take a sharp right turn to a path with the woods on your right and green open space, tennis courts and a bowling green to your left. This leads to Church Hill, the road which perhaps more than any other in the district recalls something of the former charm of rural Winchmore Hill. The view from the park gates, looking up the hill towards The Green has changed surprisingly little over the years. The appearance of Church Hill is greatly enhanced by the belt of trees separating the two sections of the road. Until the houses on the north side were built, these trees formed the boundary of Stone Hall, which stood a little to the north. This was one of the many large gentlemen's houses that existed in Winchmore Hill until well into the 20th century. On the right-hand side are **WOODSIDE COTTAGES** (Grade II GV), one of the most picturesque survivals of the old village. The middle one was the village schoolhouse until 1859 when a new school was built a little higher up the hill next to the church. This was itself replaced by the present school in Ringwood Way in 1960.

Woodside Cottages

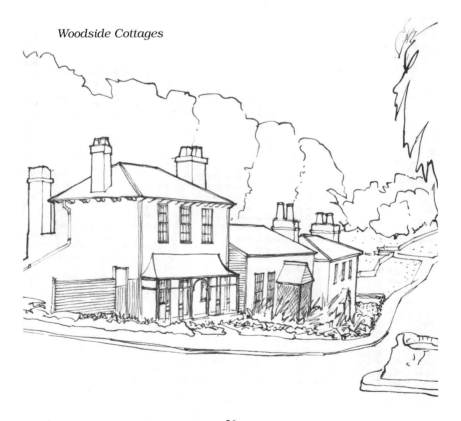

6. On the left-hand side of the hill, immediately beyond the belt of trees, is **STONE HALL LODGE** (Local Interest), the former entrance lodge to Stone Hall. The latter was built in 1872 and the foundations and cellar walls incorporated some of the stones from the old Blackfriars Bridge. The house was demolished in 1932.

7. Opposite is **ST. PAUL'S CHURCH** (Grade II), which was built in 1827 and paid for largely out of a special fund administered by the Church Building Commissioners for the erection of churches in areas of expanding population after the Napoleonic Wars. Initially St. Paul's was a "chapel of ease" to All Saints, Edmonton but later became a parish church in its own right. One of a number of so-called "Waterloo" churches dating from this period, it was built to a functional design sometimes referred to as "Churchwardens' Gothic". Next to the church, behind a high brick wall, is the spacious vicarage erected in 1913.

8. The oldest place of worship in Winchmore Hill, the **FRIENDS MEETING HOUSE** (Grade II), is a little further up the hill on the left-hand side. The earliest recorded Quaker meeting at Winchmore Hill took place in 1661 but the first meeting on the present site was held in 1676. A proper meeting house was erected in 1688 and rebuilt in its present form in 1790 as recorded on a plaque over the doorway. The low curved wall in front was designed to allow carriages to be turned when the road was very narrow at this point. The adjoining burial ground contains the graves of many well known Quakers, including members of the Barclay family of bankers. There are also gravestones for members of the Hoare family of bankers. The Quaker physician, John Fothergill and the pioneer meteorologist, Luke Howard, are buried here in unmarked graves. The CARETAKER'S COTTAGE is also Grade II listed.

9. At the top of the hill on the left is **DEVON HOUSE** (Grade II), another reminder of the old village. Originally 18th century, it was completely reconstructed in 1985.

10. The two arches to the left of the house are a modern addition, balancing the older arches to the right. This building to the right was at one time the **VILLAGE FIRE STATION**. Near ground level on the central pillar is an Ordnance Survey bench mark.

11. This building now forms part of the **KING'S HEAD PUBLIC HOUSE**, built in 1899 to replace an older inn of the same name. A stone plaque high up on the Wades Hill frontage carries the words "The King's Head and Railway Hotel" beneath the bust of a king.

12. Immediately opposite the King's Head, on the corner of The Green is a **HORSE TROUGH**, erected in 1896 in memory of Dr. Highett by the Metropolitan Drinking Fountain and Cattle Trough Association although Dr. Highett had no connection with this area. The trough has been moved from its original site near the former pond on the lower part of The Green, where the roads intersect.

13. Turn left into Wades Hill, named after John Wade, a wealthy merchant tailor who lived here in the 19th century. Wades Hill has undergone many changes, the lower part having been transformed from a country lane into a suburban street. John Wade lived at Beaumont Lodge which used to stand on the right-hand side of the road just beyond Vicars Moor Lane. Beyond the shops on the right-hand side you will see **Nos. 17-29 WADES HILL** (Grade II GV) of the late 18th or early 19th century. Nos. 23-29 are clapboard cottages which have survived almost intact except for the addition of some modern oriel windows.

14. Immediately opposite the cottages is a row of shops. Inset into the pavement in front of them are four **MANHOLE COVERS** with the wording "Wood Sanitary Engineer Winchmore Hill". Mr. Wood built some of the houses in the late 19th century terrace beyond Wades Grove.

15. At the end of the terrace stands **GLENWOOD HOUSE** (Grade II), a tall 18th century residence, part of what was once a much larger house. The right-hand portion was demolished in 1935 to make way for Keble School. Glenwood House served as the vicarage for St. Paul's Church for a period during the 19th century.

16. Just beyond Keble School take a small detour by turning left into **HAR-WOOD'S YARD** to view the compact community of 19th century houses set behind attractive front gardens and hidden from the road.

17. Continue down to Nos. 38-56 Wades Hill, a row of houses starting with Burleigh Terrace (1895). At the end of the row was the entrance to **BROADFIELDS**, home of Sir William Paulin, the brewer, a generous benefactor of the district. The house was demolished in 1931 but the stable block was retained and is now incorporated into the

Glenwood House

residential development on the corner of Wades Hill and Paulin Drive. It can just be seen behind the flats in Paulin Drive.

18. On the opposite side of this road are modern elderly folks' residences named **ESTHER DOE LODGE** because they were built on almost the same site as the almshouses erected by Esther Doe in 1868 in memory of her husband, as recorded on the plaque over the entrance which was removed from the old houses when they were demolished in 1974.

70-76 Vicars Moor Lane

19. Cross Wades Hill to enter **VICARS MOOR LANE**. Past the two semi-detached houses on the left-hand side, a range of mainly 18th and 19th century dwellings extends to the railway bridge and beyond. This forms an interesting collection of houses and cottages of varied styles which forms a separate Conservation Area. **Nos. 82-106A** are listed Local Interest. No. 106A was formerly a chapel, built in 1883 and used until 1982 by the Strict Baptists. It has been converted into a private house. No. 100 was the coach house to No. 102. Some of the houses carry fire insurance marks. Stratfield Park Close is built on the site of the railway goods yard.

20. Let into the brickwork at the further end of the bridge parapet on the right-hand side is a small **STONE ENGRAVED "JA 1879"**. This refers to John Ashley, a goods manager of the Great Northern Railway who had a large house called Vicarsmoor built just beyond the bridge. The engraved stone was preserved when the house was demolished in the late 1950s.

21. Inset into a wall bordering a service road at the side of George Parr House (the first building on the right over the bridge) is a **STONE ENGRAVED "TM"** and the date 1854. This refers to Thomas Mann who lived at Roseneath, a house that stood on this site. The Manns founded the brewing firm of Mann, Crossman and Paulin. A daughter married into the Paulin family.

22. Opposite is a substantial terrace of 19th century houses with fine porticos, **Nos. 66-76** (Grade II GV). Nos. 70-76 form an attractive terrace. No. 76, nearest the railway, retains on its windows the decorative boxes behind which the rolled canvas blinds were protected when not in use. No. 66-68A is a detached double-fronted house in the same style, now divided into four properties.

23. Further along on the right-hand side is the site of **ROSE COTTAGE**, home of the poet Thomas Hood from 1829 to 1832. The house was demolished following bomb damage during the Second World War but a portion of the boundary wall survives in the garden of No. 59. A plaque on the front of the house records the site.

Turn back across the railway bridge and take the footpath between the first two houses on the left. This leads into Wilson Street, a cul-de-sac of 19th century houses, some retaining ornamental iron brackets under their porches. At the junction of Wilson Street with Station Road you will find the railway station a few yards to the left.

Enfield Preservation Society
publications in print

Portrait of Gentleman's Row	£9.50

A History of Enfield by David Pam:

Volume I - A Parish near London (before 1837)	£16.95
Volume II - A Victorian Suburb (1837-1914)	£17.95
Volume III - A Desirable Neighbourhood (1914-39)	£18.50
Fighting for the Future by Valerie Carter	£16.95
Treasures of Enfield, editor Valerie Carter	£13.50
Enfield Footpath Map	£1.50
Enfield Quiz Book by Betty Smith	£1.50
Colour postcards – series of 20 local views	15p. each
Christmas cards – a card showing a local view or roproduction of a print is produced annually Pack of 5	£1.50
Wallet of 10 notelets (two local views)	£2.25

Other promotional items such as badges, pens etc.

*The books can be purchased from Waterstone's Bookshop,
26 Church Street, Enfield. Other retail outlets sell some books, maps
and cards. All items are available from Enfield Preservation Society,
Jubilee Hall, 2 Parsonage Lane, Enfield, EN2 OAJ*

PUBLICATIONS OF LOCAL INTEREST FROM
SOUTHGATE DISTRICT CIVIC TRUST

Winchmore Hill: Memories of a Lost Village by Henrietta Cresswell.
A reprint of 19th century childhood recollections, first published
in 1912.   **£6.00**

The Cresswells of Winchmore Hill: A Gifted Victorian Family
by Peter Hodge.
The story of a talented family and their achievements.   **£9.50**

Broomfield: An Illustrated History of the House and Garden
by Steven Brindle. A fully researched account of this historic
Palmers Green estate.   **£2.50**

Maps
Reprints of large-scale Ordnance Survey plans of the village centre:
>   *Winchmore Hill, 1865*   **£1.50**
>   *Winchmore Hill, 1896* (published by Alan Godfrey)   **£2.50**

Postcards
Coloured postcards of Southgate, Winchmore Hill and Palmers
Green:
>   *Southgate*, set of 6 cards   **£1.50**
>   *Winchmore Hill and Palmers Green*, set of 7 cards   **£1.50**
>   Early 20th century views of the district, set of 4 cards **£1.00**

Oakleaves No. 3: Local History Bulletin
Articles include: A Winchmore Hill ornithologist, the New River,
Bowes Manor, New Southgate, Stevie Smith of Palmers Green,
John Walker of Southgate.   **£5.25**

*Prices include postage and packing, and are correct at time of
going to press. Publications available from Southgate District Civic
Trust, 64 Houndsden Road, Winchmore Hill, London N21 1LY.*

ENFIELD PRESERVATION SOCIETY, founded in 1936, aims to protect Enfield's historic heritage, defend the green belt and encourage good design in new developments. It has a long record of vigorous activity in defence of the natural and built environment and many of the buildings mentioned in these walks have survived thanks to intervention by EPS. A regular programme of meetings, walks and outings is organised for members (who number 2000+). Membership enquiries are welcome and should be addressed to EPS, Jubilee Hall, 2 Parsonage Lane, Enfield, EN2 0AJ. Details of current activities can be viewed on the society's website, *www.enfieldpressoc.org.uk*

SOUTHGATE DISTRICT CIVIC TRUST is a voluntary amenity society for the Southgate district. It was founded in 1962 to promote the conservation and enhancement of the best aspects of the district. This includes the monitoring of local planning applications. The Trust has successfully campaigned for the creation of Conservation Areas, building preservation and protection of the natural environment. Details of activities and publications are available from Mr. G. Bone, The Tower, Quakers Walk, London, N21 2DE or from local libraries.